Getting Paid Using Social Media 2

Part of the Collecting Money Series

By Michelle Dunn

www.michelledunn.com
www.credit-and-collections.com

Cover design by
WoW! Graphic Designs www.wowgraphicdesigns.com

This book is designed to provide accurate and authoritative information in regard to the subject matter covered. It is sold with the understanding that the author is not engaged in rendering legal advice or services. If legal advice is required, please see your attorney.

Disclaimer

This book is designed to provide information to help you learn more about collecting money from past due customers. It is sold with the understanding that the publisher and author are not giving legal, accounting, or other professional advice or services. The content of this book is based upon my own personal research and experience. If legal or other assistance is required, please see your attorney or accountant.

Every effort has been made to make this book as accurate as possible. However, there may be mistakes. This book is sold as a guide with what information is current as of the date of the original printing.

Please note: Every effort has been made to assure this information is up to date and accurate as of publication date. It is not intended to be a full and exhaustive explanation of the law in any area. This information is not intended as legal or financial advice and may not be used as legal or financial advice. Please consult with your attorney, tax professional, and state and federal agencies to verify information for your individual situation.

Foreword

Social media has taken over the internet – 95% of people who use the internet also belong to at least one social network, and most belong to more than one. Many of those people spend a good amount of time sharing on those social networks. They share photos, relationship information, daily grind information, work and employment information, stories about their pets, kids and families; they share videos, brag about new jobs, pay raises and new cars, boats, vacations and clothes.

This book is to help business owners, entrepreneurs, and credit managers use that information to their advantage to learn more about their customers and improve their collections and recovery of bad debts for their business. This book can also be used by bill collectors who are trying to gather and verify information on customers who are avoiding them, and to get their clients invoices paid.

Social media is a great, public, free tool for anyone who wants to know anything about anyone who participates. There are many ways to utilize these networks to benefit your business and to help you get paid, all within the boundaries of the law.

Table of Contents

Introduction

Hi, my name is Michelle Dunn and I wrote this book based on all the questions my readers have been sending me about getting paid and how they can utilize social media to help them do that. I knew this was an important topic when I started getting calls from the Federal Trade Commission's attorney's asking me questions about how business owners and bill collectors were using social media, email, cell phones and text messages as part of their collection efforts. What I hope to achieve with this book is to be able to bring new bill collectors (these could be business owners, accounts receivable clerks, or credit managers – even third party collectors) up to speed quickly on how they can effectively and ethically use social media as part of their credit processes.

I think it is important to help collectors and businesses understand the risks of using social media so they can take precautions to avoid those risks and shorten the curve for implementing new policies and procedures as the laws are changed. I also want you to understand and implement the best business practices for utilizing social media in collections. This book will help guide you through new technology questions based on existing and Federal laws as well as helping you to create a workplace culture where collectors apply new information as the laws are changed and updated. Social media changes every day – even as I write this it is changing – it is important for you to understand it to be able to use it to your advantage.

"Don't post anything online that you wouldn't want your grandmother to read" – anonymous

Finding people online...it's easier than you think

Most people use social networking websites more than regular email nowadays, 95% of people who use the internet belong to at least one social network. Social networking websites are a venue for people to share personal or business information with other people through a web site that is specifically designed to make it easy to share text, pictures, documents, music, videos and other data and comments. There are thousands of social networking websites out there today and more every day. Some focus on specific industries, interests, subjects or topics. Members can join for free and create a profile and add anything they would like, as well as connect with other like minded people who are also members.

Many businesses use social networks to find out information about their customers since many consumers and businesses now have public profile pages on social media websites and you can find things such as a mailing address, phone number, cell phone number, place of employment and other information by looking at those sites. You can also find information in search engines, on blogs, message boards, posted videos, newsgroups and photos, as well as through free services such as Google alerts or Google map.

When you use social media in regards to your customers you will be using it as a viewing experience rather than an interactive experience. Meaning that you should never message, post, or request friendship from a customer that you are collecting from and are using social media to verify or gather information to help you do that.

Twitter, Facebook, MySpace or LinkedIn may help you locate someone, however, using any one of those websites' to announce any type of pending or ongoing collection activity could violate privacy laws, state collection laws and if you are a third party collector the FDCPA.

Another great tool to help you find out information is to use Google. You can do a search on Google or set up a "Google Alerts". Google alerts are great, easy, free and convenient. You can set up a Google alert for a person, and Google will send you an email each time that name is mentioned somewhere on the web. Many newspapers, local and national now have their newspapers available online and you will get an email if that name is mentioned in any story, anywhere. Remember to put the first and last name with quotation marks as your Google alert to make sure you only receive alerts for that specific name.

So what exactly IS social media? Social media is websites where people meet others, start and participate in conversations and become part of a community. It is a venue for people to publish thoughts, comments, documents, or anything they wish with the ability to share it with others and network to grow their "friends" or followers and expand their network or reach.

Online Collection techniques are skills and techniques used by collectors on the internet to locate debtors or past due customers in order to then try and collect on a debt by traditional means.

Some examples of types of online collection websites other than social media websites would be skip tracing websites public records websites, court records, or anything online that can help a collector locate a debtor.

Consumer credit is a critical part of our economy, good or bad. Credit allows consumers to purchase goods and services for which they are unable or unwilling to pay for at the time of purchase. By extending credit to those people, you are taking a risk that this person may not be able to pay you back part or all of the money they now owe you. You need to use everything that is legally available to you to ensure that you get paid.

Demographics

Many social media sites are geared towards certain audiences, for example, LinkedIn is more for business people, and MySpace is more artists, musicians or younger people. If your customers are under 30 years old, or artists or may be "hanging out" on MySpace, then that is the social network you may want to keep an eye on. Those same people may not be on a social site such as LinkedIn. According to the May/June 2011 issue of Book Business, 51% of Americans ages 12 and older have a Facebook profile, up from 8% in 2008 and only 8% of those surveyed use Twitter.

In my opinion anyone who puts personal information on a public website would have no expectation of privacy since if what they were posting were private; they would not be posting it. Many of the people who use these social media websites, whether they owe debts or not have never read any of these social websites privacy notices and are naïve when it comes to privacy expectations. Everyone who posts something online on a public website or profile page leaves a digital footprint on the internet that can always be found. It is up to the poster to use common sense, for example if you don't owe anyone money and post every private aspect of your life online, you won't have a problem. The folks that post private information online AND owe money to people, those are the folks that are unhappy. I do have to say I am always very surprised at the amount of information you can find on these social websites. You would think that with this in the news so much that more people who owe money and are using these websites would have their accounts set to private or stop posting such personal information.

Some of the things you find online can help you be more effective as you use the internet and social media websites to search for information. Using social media or search engines can help you locate a hard to find customer, it can help you much better if you segment and prioritize your past due accounts and you can also tailor your efforts by the "type" of debt you are trying to collect and make more educated decisions.

Locating & Tracking Customers/Debtors Using Social Media

Consumers everywhere are upset that collectors are utilizing social networks to locate them in order to collect a debt. Many are claiming this is unethical and just another "low life tactic" to harass a customer. Let us remember a customer becomes a debtor when they owe someone money. Unfortunately, many debtors believe that if their financial situation changes or if they over spend, they should not have to pay that money back and get upset when they are contacted by a business or collector who is trying to get paid.

On September 28th, 2009 the NYDaily News ran a story by Tripp Whetsell called "Collection firms join old pals looking for you on Facebook", They tell the story of Michael Bucello who got his first credit card in college and who then had trouble resisting the urge to use that card when shopping. He racked up over $1,600.00 on his credit card and then had trouble paying so he shredded the card but never paid the bill. His reason for never paying the bill was that he had received several notices about the debt but then presumed as the years went by that his old debt had been forgotten.

This is a common story and excuse from debtors;

they think that if they ignore a debt, it will go away. Obviously, if you don't pay a bill, it is still out there. Much like situations we don't want to face in life, we think if we ignore it, it will go away – and as we know – that isn't what happens, it just makes the situation worse! Bucello is now upset that a debt collector noticed his Facebook page and that collection activities have resumed. When his bank account was frozen he decided to make good on the debt. He did go on to say that he is a lot more vigilant about what he does on the internet but that he also got a crash course about the importance of paying his bills on time.

With the advancement of technology, social media is a tool used by businesses, banks, skip tracers and debt collectors to obtain, verify, and analyze information regarding their customers. The Associated Press recently reported that Facebook will save user profiles of deceased people. This means that if you are looking for a customer that is deceased, and you find their Facebook profile, you will instead see a memorial profile which will differ from a normal Face-book profile. Facebook will delete contact information from memorial profiles and block people from logging into the deceased persons' account. You can use this information to close out an account or pursue the estate once you verify the person is actually deceased.

The state Internal Revenue Service has a new tool in social media as well. They mine information from Facebook and MySpace and authorities in Minnesota, Nebraska, California and other states have been able to successfully collect back taxes according to a report in the Wall Street Journal. They look for a wide variety of information to help them collect such as relocation announcements, earnings boats, gig announcements and more.

I recently read that a Nebraska tax official, Steven Schroeder indicated to the Wall Street Journal that using a Google search is often the first step when they can't find a tax evader. If a Google search doesn't return any results they visit social media networking websites and online chat rooms. Some states, one of them being Massachusetts, aren't using social media sites to locate tax evaders, though spokespeople for Wisconsin and Oregon indicated that they are actively looking into it. Many other states are looking into using social media for tax audits, negotiations and collections.

Some collection attorney's or process servers say they have used the pictures people post on Facebook or MySpace to help them get a physical description or a person so they can serve them with legal paperwork.

Some of the things you can find posted online through social networks that can help you as a collector:

Birth date, address, employment information, phone numbers, home phone #, work #, cell #, asset information and more.

With a name and a birth date a collector can then search public records on an individual. A collector I know sifts through pictures on social media websites and runs license plates that they find in those photos for clues as to where the debtor may be living. She said 1 in 10 are truthful about their employment and end up talking about their lives on their profile pages giving you enough information to plan your next collection effort or repossession move.

Facebook

Many people have asked me what do you find on these social networking websites, many of you are not familiar with these websites and don't know where to look or what you are looking for. I will start with Facebook, one of the more popular social media websites. If you visit a profile of someone on Facebook and you are their friend or they don't have their information set to private some of the things you can find out include:

What I look like

My current city and state

My friends – you can see if I work with any of them to get a possible place of employment

Links to other social networks I participate in

Links to my blog or personal website

My status or my updates – which can include when I spend money, get a new job, buy a house or get a raise or bonus

You can then click on the tabs at the top of the profile for more information, for example, if you click on Info, you can possibly find out my hometown city and state, my siblings or relatives, my email address, my physical or mailing address, my employer and where they are located and possible their website address. If you click on Photo's, you can see all kinds of pictures of me and my family and friends, so if you are trying to serve me any legal papers, now you know what I look like. If you click on the Plus Sign, you can see my links, events and notes. Not everyone fills all of this information out but you will be surprised at how many do in great detail.

Many of you who read this book or attend my webinar about Using Social Media in Collections ask about Facebooks Privacy policy and how it affects you and how you use it in this capacity. Make sure to read Facebooks updated privacy policy –as of this writing it was last updated on April 26, 2011. (http://www. facebook.com/terms.php)

Something else worth mentioning is that in December 2008, the Supreme Court of the Australian Capital Territory rules that Facebook is a valid protocol to serve court notices to defendants. It is believed to be the world's first legal judgment that defines a summons posted on Facebook as legally binding.

In March 2008, the New Zealand High Court associate justice David Glendall allowed for the serving of legal papers on Craig Axe by the company Axe Market Garden via Facebook.

One collector said he was able to collect from a debtor who had returned to Japan after he located him on Facebook. Some other collectors have told me that they don't have much luck using social media websites and the most they seem to get are possible places of employment and birth dates. Another agency owner said he has had to fire collectors who have contacted debtors through social media websites; the lure is strong especially when payments are down.

A judgment recovery professional said he was working on a judgment and the judgment debtor had a unique name so he Googled it. It turned out the judgment debtor had a Facebook account, the collector thought the debtor may have included work friends under his Facebook friends and so he Googled one of the judgment debtors friends. He found out where that person worked on his first try. He then Googled the work place and found a web page with a phone number, it was after hours so when he called he got the afterhours message and one of the options was to hear the extension list. He listened and his debtor was listed on the extension list. Having more or less verifying employment he was able to initiate garnishment. He has never heard from the judgment debtor but the payments are being made. This proves that skip tracing and investigative work is possible using social networks, without "friending" a debtor or breaking the law.

Facebook now has a reverse email search option that can also help you find people if you have an email address. I tried it by typing an email address in the search box at the top of Facebooks home page and the marching profile shows up.

Another collector that I know said she read somewhere that businesses, banks and collectors are using Facebook as a search tool by looking through pictures and looking for any that may have been taken at a debtors job or workplace and they look for the name of the business in the background of the pictures, or at the "work" shirts or cap the debtor may be wearing that bear the company name.

Social networking is all the rage. People today think nothing of posting personal information, with their location for anyone to see. People use Facebook to share news about new jobs, the loss of jobs, relocations, their achievements, their children's achievements, their political views, purchases, vacations and post pictures of everything they do and in some cases what they eat!

MySpace

When you visit MySpace and search for the name of a customer, make sure to try and narrow your search by using the form on the right hand side where you can put in the city and state if you have it, zip code, gender, age and more. There are many people with the same name and you need to make sure you always have the right person. When you visit someone's profile on MySpace you will immediately see a picture of them, and next to that picture, many times is listed their age, gender, city, state and country. You can read what they have written about themselves and their lives. This can include any job information, or tell you if they own anything or are moving, buying a car, or anything that is happening in their life. This can help you when you are making collection calls because if what they tell you marches what you see on their MySpace page they are probably telling you the truth. If you keep looking down the left hand side of a profile you can also find their occupation and this can help you if you are in search for a place of employment. You can also find out their education and employment history if they filled that portion of their profile out.

Twitter

Twitter is a social networking website where people can share and discover what is happening right now, anywhere in the world. When Twitter first began, it was more social and fun but now more and more businesses are joining the Twitter network. Twitter allows anyone who signs up the ability to send and read messages, known as tweets. Tweets are text posts of up to 140 characters displayed on that user's profile page and the pages of their followers. Most people use Twitter to communicate or keep in touch with friends or family, telling them what they are doing "right now", where they are and to ask questions.

Using Twitter to locate a customer that owes you money can provide you with a photo of that customer, a city and state, and possibly a website if they have one, or maybe an employer's website. You can read their tweets to see what they are doing, for example, are they looking for a job, buying a new car, going through bankruptcy?

You can search for people's names on the twitter website but there are also other ways to search for people on Twitter. The Twitter people search isn't the best way to find people on Twitter but it is a good start, just click on "Find People" on the Twitter home page at the very top and type in the name of the person you are looking for.

You can also use a website such as Tweepz, which lets you limit searches to specific parts of Twitter's user information, such as name, bio, and location. You can also filter results by follower/following numbers, location, and other terms, and greatly improve your results.

Another Twitter search tool is called TweepSearch, which lets you search by Twitter name or location, or search a specific username.

Contacting Customers Using Social Networks

Stop for a moment before you decide to "contact" a customer in any way on a social media website. One collection agency that is a member of my discussion group contacted a debtor through MySpace and ended up being sued (and rightfully so!). Something I should mention is that if you do decide to use social media to message or contact a customer in any way, the social network would not be liable, they would have immunity under Section 230 of the Communications Decency Act, but you as the collection agency owner, would be responsible. If you were the owner of a business that did this, you would be responsible, even if it was one of your employees that made the contact or post. As a debt collector you may not publicize a debt or discuss a debt with anyone else other than the debtor, their spouse or an attorney, so using a social network to communicate with a debtor would fall into this category. Many news articles that I have been reading lately seem to think that credit managers, business owners or collectors that utilize social networks to locate a customer that owes them money is a "bad" practice. Many of these articles state that debt collectors are pretending to be "hot" girls in order to "friend" a customer and trick them into paying. While this may be going on at some seedy collection agencies, this has not been my experience in talking to a majority of business owners, credit managers, accounts receivable clerks or collectors. In view of this, I suggest you do utilize social networks to locate customers that owe you money but also to verify information you may already have, to make sure you have the correct person or customer before making contact, and then making contact by phone or through the mail. Never using the email or contact feature on a social networking website.

This all seems to be common sense and most of the collectors and credit people I talk to feel the same way. As we know the debt collection industry and collectors in general have a bad reputation based on a handful of agencies or collectors that break the law and then are featured in news stories. This has been going on for so many years and only gets worse as more consumers get into more debt. So as long as you act ethically and follow your common sense, keep a paper trail and keep an eye on your employees, you won't have any problems.

Dos & Don'ts of Using Social Media in Collections

As a first party collector you do not need to follow the FDCPA but you should be aware of it and make yourself familiar with it. The FDCPA and the FCRA don't specifically talk about what you can or cannot do online since when these laws were enacted, there wasn't any of the new technology we all use today. If you read these Acts you can apply them to social media by using some common sense. Here are some things to think about when utilizing the internet for your debt collections:

Skip tracing or locating debtors
Accepting customer payments
Researching collection tools, such as software or skip tracing tools
Credit reporting
Use database technology to maintain account information on customers that owe you money
Researching place of employment
Verifying information you already have on a customer

Don't use the internet for:

Emailing a debtor about a debt if you are a third party collector

Sending debt collection emails, faxes or text messages

Don't send a "friend request" to a debtor on any social networking website, ever.

Never converse with a debtor using a social media website by utilizing the email or comment feature.

Do not email a debtor about a debt if you think a third party could ever read that email

Texting

If you DO email debtors or past due customers and they don't respond to your email, stop emailing them and try to reach them through traditional methods, which would be by phone or postal mail.

Never publish a list of names of debtors any where online

When Congress enacted the FDCPA, they did not limit the methods a debt collector could use to contact a consumer except for prohibiting the use of postcards but this was before any new technology. However, it is important to remember that the FDCPA was enacted to prevent debt collectors from

engaging in unfair, deceptive or abusive conduct in using any method to collect a debt.
New technology raises questions and issues not considered when the FDCPA was enacted.

The FDCPA applies to third party collectors; business owners should check their specific state laws to see what they can or cannot do. Many state laws mirror the FDCPA.

Something you can do is utilize social networking sites to locate or find a debtor; get a mailing address or employment information in order to enforce any in-house collections. With a place of employment a creditor can better evaluate someone's ability to pay and if you're in the position to attach assets, you would then be able to garnish pay if state laws allow. Creditors can use database technology to maintain the account information of customers to whom they have already extended credit. For example, if you are a member of one of the credit bureaus, you can utilize many online services they provide that can help you collect. Credit bureaus offer services such as skip tracing tools, address updates, segmentation tools, and more.

The Federal Trade Commission enforces the FDCPA and is aware that changes need to be made in order to bring the Act up to date in regards to new technology among other things.

I would like to share with you my top 4 tips of what you can do to have more success using social networks to locate debtors, and better your business:

Everyone is doing it, this is one time when you should follow the pack and participate.

Listen, just like any other networking event, listen before you "talk"

Track conversations with keywords, names, company names, executives names and use Google Reader and Google Blog Search (both free) to track them.

Practice participating in social medias so that you understand how they work. Many people, who might be a debtor, spend hours on these websites and know them inside and out.

Text messages and Email

As a creditor text messages and emails seem to be the preferred and most effective way to increase collections. One company I know has experienced a 12 percent lift in communication by using text messages and email. It seems that email or a text message as an avenue of communication is perceived as less evasive than a phone call, and your customer has the sense of being in control of when and if they respond.

Some collectors I have spoken with obtain consent from their customers before the sale for text messages to be used for future correspondence. They include this wording on the paperwork the customer signs when opening an account, such as the credit application, agreement or contract. The wording is similar to this:

"By signing this document, customer agrees to accept and understands that text messages may be used when servicing their account, including the collecting of debts."

Others have taken it a step further and have a more detailed outline of how text messages will be used. They always get the customer to sign and acknowledge this provision:

"You authorize us (your company name) to send you (customer name) a text message at any mobile number at which we reasonable believe we can contact you, for any lawful purpose, including but not limited to:

1. *Suspected fraud or identity theft*
2. *Obtaining information necessary to service your account*
3. *Collecting on your account*
4. *Notifying you to important issues regarding your account"*

Something important to remember if you are thinking of doing this, all messages include a mechanism for the consumer to opt out of receiving further text messages at any time. This is to protect the consumer and the collector, especially since the law does not specifically address text messages being sent as a form of dunning. If you decide to send text messages about bills to your customers, make sure the customer is not charged for the text and that you as the company, incur that charge.

Consider that some cell phones that accept text messages may be "business" phones or provided by a consumers employer, that employer may have the right to view any text messages sent to or received by that company phone. This would violate third party disclosure through the FDCPA. Also, many consumers have phones that multiple family members may use and they could see a message from you that is for their sibling or parent.

Another consideration with text messages is how much space are you going to use to include the mini-miranda or your collection information? It may be difficult to include any legal information along with a debt collection notice on a text message.

You might want to take a look at the Telephone Consumer Protection Act (TCPA) since their requirements may also apply to text messages. The TCPA prohibits any call using any type of automated dialing telephone system to any number assigned through a cellular telephone service. If you are using an automatic dialer, be sure to verify you aren't breaking any laws.

To avoid getting into trouble there are some steps you can take to protect yourself but not completely since the law is not entirely clear on this issue:

- Obtain consent from the consumer in writing to communicate via email or text
- Clearly state in your emails or text messages that you are a bill collector
- Include your phone number
- Provide opt-out information so a consumer can STOP any emails or text messages
- Use "Free to end user" services so debtors or consumers never incur a charge for your messages.

The Risks of Using Social Media as a Collection Tool

Many people new to the collection industry don't realize the implications of third party disclosure and how it affects the industry, the collectors and the consumers in the long run. On March 31, 2009, Ryan Singel wrote a story titled "Woman sues debt collectors for "MySpace posting". According to Singel, a consumer fell behind on her payments in early January on her 2005 Chevy Impala, the last thing she wanted to do was share that information on her MySpace profile or any other social networking website. But that's just what the debt collector assigned to her debt did. This woman then filed a civil lawsuit against the collection agency accusing them of violating collections law by harassing her online, on the phone and in person. She asked for $25,000.00 in damages.

The court found that because of the post to her MySpace page, she suffered damage to her business and community reputation, extreme mental distress, aggravation, humiliation and embarrassment.

Under most state laws, debt collectors may not publicize a debt or even tell a debtor's friends, family members, or co-workers about a debt in order to shame a person into paying. Collectors must also refrain from using abusive or oppressing methods, and generally have to stop calling a debtors home or work after being asked to communicate only in writing.

Social websites are a tool, just like a credit report is a tool to you as a collector. As a collector this information is to be viewed only, to verify information you already have and not for any other purpose and without contacting the debtor through that medium.

When you use a social networking website to locate a debtor, to then try to collect from them using the phone or mail, there normally won't be a problem. The problems start when a collector contacts a debtor through one of these social websites. Since the information, messages or conversations on these types of websites is not private and is available to many people to see, this would not be a tool to use as part of your debt collection effort without violating Federal laws specifically applicable to consumer debt collections. Most of these types of web-sites are integrated with electronic mail and you can send email to one specific person, BUT, just how private is this? How can you be sure? Better safe than sorry – don't use the email tools on these websites to contact someone who owes money.

If a customer contacts you through email or a text and asks you to contact them through a social media networking website or through any other electronic means not covered by the existing debt collection laws, I would advise against it. Some agencies are doing this if they have the original email or text from the customer so that they can print it out and bring it with them to court if they are sued. Others are not utilizing new technology to contact customers about past due bills until the laws are changed.

I would like to share some social media myths with you that can help you to be more successful in your efforts.

It's a passing fad. Social media is here to stay and growing by the day.

It is something you can control. Social media is controlled by the users, not the viewers; you can only control your reaction.

It's a one-time set up. Once you create a profile or join a social media web-site, you cannot just set up a profile and leave it. You must be active and log into your account. Social media is something you have to work at and keep learning about for it to be effective for you.

There are no rules. Some people believe that they can do and say whatever they want without consequences.

Laws & Regulations

If you are in the debt collection business you are always following laws and regulations, learning about laws and regulations, trying to get new laws passed, making sure your collectors are following those laws and basically fearing the reaper. When I recently asked members of my discussion group, what debt collection laws and regulations are on your minds right now as you try to collect and get new customers in this recession, the top response was: "The laws and regulations need to be updated and reviewed with changes to reflect the times in order for collectors to effectively do their jobs and do them well. Collectors have a hard job even more so now with the economy in a down turn. Having unclear laws and regulations only makes their job tougher.

As collectors look for ways to communicate with debtors effectively, they are realizing that they have to "listen" more and talk less; they are focusing on proactive ways to work with debtors to avoid conflicts in the first place. It is also imperative that collectors learn how to collect during a recession from customer's who may not have jobs, may have lost their homes and re struggling now more than ever before. Being up to date on laws and regulations is imperative to collectors during these tough times, learning how to set up realistic payment arrangements, following through and working with debtors is one of the only ways to get paid when debtors have little money to spare.

Collectors also see a rise in law suits and are looking for lawmakers to make decisions, one way or the other, but to just make a decision and stick to it so the collection industry can go about their business. According to the Federal Trade Commission, the FTC workshop in Chicago discussed collection litigation practices and policy issues surrounding the accounts receivable management industry's use of the legal system. This event follows up on a 2009 report by the FTC Collecting Consumer Debts: The Challenges of Change, which recommended that the debt collection regulatory system in the U.S. should be reformed and modernized.

This is great news for industry professionals that feel the FTC has been non-committal about many regulations and laws, making a collector's job harder than it already is. For example, the FTC has been unclear as to what constitutes the appropriate authorization to use a mobile phone for debt collections. This is tough because land lines are becoming a thing of the past as more people use cell phones exclusively. In order to work with debtors collectors must be able to communicate with them.

On February 26, 2009 the FTC issued a report recommending that the debt collection legal system be changed to reflect changes in the debt collection industry. The report described the changes the FTC believes will provide better consumer protection without unduly burdening the debt collection industry. According to this report, debt collection laws should be modernized to reflect changes in technology.

What comes to mind is that many states have debt collection laws that mirror the FDCPA. States may need to modify their laws to also reflect the modern times and the need for fair debt collection. Only with all of these changes will debt collection be fair.

Collectors provide a valuable service to business owners everywhere, what makes their job hard is not having clear cut rules to follow, and having gray areas that cause emotionally distressed debtors who may also be depressed and upset that they are struggling to lash out at a bill collector who contacts them. With the laws the way they are it is not uncommon for a debtor to sue a collector for a violation that may or may not be valid, but ultimately suing to get out of paying a debt that they rightfully owe. According to the FTC, they received more than 78,000 complaints about third-party debt collectors in 2009. While this is a small decrease in the number of complaints received in 2007, the FTC continues to receive more complaints about debt collectors than any other industry.

Being a proactive collector in these times is a must for every collector out there. Only you can help change how the laws and regulations impact your job and therefore your job performance.

Resources

Full 120 page February 2009 FTC
Workshop Report:
www.ftc.gov/bcp/workshops/debtcollecti
on/dcwr.pdf

Where collectors connect online:
www.collectiontechnology.net/

My Credit & Collections Blog:
www.Credit-and-Collections.com

Business to Business online debt collection letters
service: Ecollectionletters.com

Help getting paid that works with your existing
accounting software: www.ZenCash.com

Need a collection agency for your business?
http://collectiondynamics.com

Tweepz – online twitter search tool:
www.tweepz.com Another online twitter search
tool: http://tweepsearch.com

Yet another online twitter search tool: www.twellow.com

Public Records Information online: www.publicrecordsinfo.com

Public Records Finder: www.publicrecordfinder.com

Free Federal Court Dockets: www.freecourtdockets.com

Find birthdates: www.birthdatabase.com

Social Security Number Validator: www.ssnvalidator.com

Search for blog posts: www.whostalkin.com

Search twitter postings: http://search.twitter.com

Collections and Credit Risk http://www.collectionscreditrisk.com/

Collection Industry News
http://collectionindustrynews.com/

Credit and Collections News
http://www.creditandcollectionnews.com/blog.php

Credit Management Association
http://creditmanagementassociation.org/category/nacm/

CUCollector http://blog.cucollector.com/

Elm Street Economy
http://www.elmstreeteconomy.com/

Michelle Dunn's columns on Entrepreneur
http://www.entrepreneur.com/author/127

FDCPA Certification:
http://www.fdcpacertification.com

Skip tracing: Pick up the book "Manhunt" by Ron Brown

Networking groups: Starting a Collection Agency, moderated by Michelle Dunn

http://www.linkedin.com/groups/Starting-Collection-Agency-2320092?gid=2320092&trk=hb_side_g

Articles

FFIEC Issues Social Media Guidance, seeks feedback
By Mary Wisniewski Jan. 22, 2013
Published in American Banker

Increased use of Social Media by Debt Collectors reported
By Stuart Lieberman, a New Horizon Credit Counseling
Published on PRWeb

Debt Collector calling...and emailing...and texting?
By Connie Prater February 27, 2008
Published by CreditCards.com

Can Debt Collectors contact you via Social Media?
By Susan Johnston
February 13, 2012
Published in US News and World Report

Are Debt Collectors your "Friends?"

Social Networks and Debt Collection, June 3, 2011, article by Law Offices of Robert M. Gellar PA *www.attorneyfortampabay.com,* press release.

Debt Collection Technology Firms await FDCPA clarity by Cynthia Wilson on May 19, 2011 for Inside ARM -

http://www.insidearm.com/daily/collectionlaws-regulations/collection-laws-and-regulations/debt-collection-technologyfirms-await-fdcpa-clarity/

The Credit Policy Workbook: a step-by-step, easy, fill in the blanks guide (The Collecting Money Series)

This workbook was created because of the many people who ask me for help in creating their credit policy. Many of you are confused by all the books out there or the explanations and need a quick, easy way to limit your credit risk by having some type of policies or an outline of how you want your cash to flow throughout your business.

It is my hope that this workbook will revolutionize how many business owners who will have a working credit policy for their business moving forward. I hope this workbook makes it easy for you to know your mission, goals and what outcome you want for your cash. With the easy to understand text and easy to fill out worksheets, I hope you have a credit policy for your business when you are done with this book. You have taken a big step towards smoother cash flow by reading this book.

Understanding the Fair Debt Collection
Practices Act (The Collecting Money Series)

Keep on track with your collections efforts, and avoid FDCPA violations.

This short easy to understand book by Michelle Dunn, Understanding and Following the Fair Debt Collection Practices Act, can help.

Many of my consulting clients and new agency owners use this as a training guide for their new collectors.

As the economy falters and the credit crisis continues help keep your business out of a lawsuit by better understanding and learning more about the Fair Debt Collection Practices Act, who is affected, what debts are covered, who enforces it and how you can collect more money while following the law.

Failing to properly train collectors is a top reason companies get sued. Don't let this happen to you! Learn as much as you can about what constitutes a violation of the FDCPA and how you can avoid making those mistakes.

Choosing the Right Collection Agency for your Business (The Collecting Money Series)

With all the bad press about collection agencies how do you decide which one to use or if you should use one at all? This short report will help business owners make an educated decision about which collection agency they want representing their business and the most efficient ways to work with an agency to get the best return.

I also talk about the red flags that can tell you that you need a collection agency, signs to look for, what to expect and how using a collection agency can affect your business.

Failing to have a collection agency hired and ready to collect on your past due accounts before it is needed is the biggest mistake business owners make in collections. This short report is critical for anyone who needs to hire a collection agency but doesn't know how to do it or what to look for.

Check out my free webinar and power point presentation to help you choose the right collection agency for your business: http://www.collectionstrainingresource.com/free30/Choose-Collection-Agency

About the author

In 1998, when Michelle was getting a divorce and had 2 small children, she started a collection agency from home leaving her full time job 6 months later. Her agency did very well and grew over the next 8 years until Michelle sold it to write full time. Michelle knew what business owners needed and had already written a couple of books that were selling well. "But it was still a huge leap", she says, "I was a single mom with two sons." I started putting together my ideas, set up an office in my home, and used the income from book sales to fund publishing more books.

That same year Michelle self published 4 books and e-books before landing her first book contract with Entrepreneur Press to write The Ultimate Credit and Collections Handbook, the check IS in the mail. She then self published a couple more business books before getting a book deal with John Wiley & Sons Publishing for her first hardcover book, The Guide to Getting Paid, weed out bad paying customers, collect on past due balances, and avoid bad debt.

Today Michelle Dunn continues to write columns and books and presents webinars sharing how business owners can limit credit risk in this economy as well as learn how they can prevent some bad debt, and collect from past due customers.

To learn more, visit MichelleDunn.com and Credit-and-Collections.com

Most books are now also available for your Kindle!

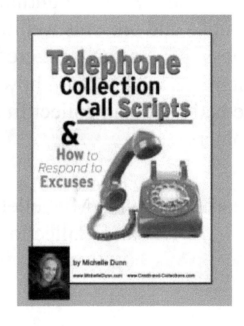